HYMNS OF THE FAITHFUL SERIES

BAPTISM
COMMUNION

LEADERS GUIDE

WRITTEN BY

Richard Resch

CPH.
Concordia Publishing House

Contents

HYMN 1

All Who Believe and Are Baptized   *Page 4*

HYMN 2

Dearest Jesus, We Are Here   *Page 6*

HYMN 3

Draw Near and Take the Body of the Lord   *Page 7*

HYMN 4

I Come, O Savior, to Your Table   *Page 9*

HYMN 5

Let All Mortal Flesh Keep Silence   *Page 11*

HYMN 6

Soul, Adorn Yourself with Gladness   *Page 12*

Series editor: Thomas J. Doyle

This publication is available in braille and in large print for the visually impaired. Write to the Library for the Blind, 1333 S. Kirkwood Rd., St. Louis, MO 63122-7295; or call 1-800-433-3954.

Introduction

The Hymns of the Faithful Bible study series provides participants the opportunity to study in-depth favorite hymns and Christian songs.

The leaders guide includes background information concerning the text and tune for some of Christendom's most beloved hymns. Each session in the leaders guide includes the following sections:

- **Textual Source(s)**–provides the scriptural sources the author used in writing the hymn.
- **The Hymn's Text**–provides information concerning the author of the hymn and the context in which the hymn was written.
- **The Hymn's Tune**–provides information concerning the tune associated with the hymn, including who wrote the tune and alternate uses of the tune.
- **Tradition about the Hymn**–describes the way in which the hymn has been used by the church.
- **The Confession of Faith Sung in This Hymn**–describes the theological truth(s) that the hymn confesses.

The study sheets are designed for use in a class or small-group setting, but may also be used by individuals for their personal devotions. Each session has a separate study sheet. Each of the study sheets includes activities and questions to guide the participant into an understanding of the basic theological truths confessed in the hymn and to assist the participant in applying these truths to life. Each study sheet includes the following sections:

- **Focus**–introduces the participant to the concepts that will be explored during the session.
- **Inform**–provides questions to guide the participant into a deeper understanding of the scriptural truths confessed in the words of the hymn. This section may be supplemented by the leader with information found in the leaders guide.
- **Connect**–provides activities and questions to help the participant apply the truth found in the words of the hymn to life.
- **Vision**–suggests activities for further devotional use of the hymn during the week to come.

In addition to the leaders guide and the study sheets, an audio CD includes a musical, sing-along version of the hymn. Use the audio CD to accompany your class or small group in singing the hymn at the beginning of each session. You may also want to play the hymn as participants arrive and/or depart from class.

May God bless the study of His Word proclaimed in the words of some of the church's favorite hymns.

Session 1

All Who Believe and Are Baptized

Textual Sources: Mark 16:16; Romans 6:3–5; Colossians 2:12–13

The Hymn's Text

"All Who Believe and Are Baptized" is one of the treasured Baptism hymns in Denmark, Norway, and the United States. It was first published in Thomas Kingo's hymnal of 1689. Kingo eventually came to be known in Denmark as the "Poet of Eastertide" because so many of his hymns were about the resurrection. When the Danish people realized that Kingo's work had exceptional merit, they made him a member of the nobility and gave him an honorary doctor of theology degree. The king then appointed him to prepare a hymnbook for the Church of Denmark. But when Kingo's hymnal came out, it met with a storm of criticism; of the 267 hymns included, 136 were by Kingo. A new person was appointed to oversee a revised hymnal. The result did not include one Kingo hymn; however, this book was not accepted either. A new commission was asked to try again and their result included 85 of Kingo's original hymns. This book was accepted.

The following epitaph was written on Kingo's monument at Odense. It was penned by Nikolai Grundtvig, the famous author of "Built On The Rock":

Thomas Kingo is the psalmist
Of the Danish temple choir.
This his people will remember
As long as song their hearts inspire.

Translation

The English translation was prepared for *The Lutheran Hymnary* (1913) by George T. Rygh. Virtually all of the present hymnal versions have been altered.

The Hymn's Tune

Unfortunately the composer of this vibrant, sturdy tune, ES IST DAS HEIL, is unknown. It appeared in *Achtliederbuch* (1524), the first Lutheran hymnal. There it was the tune for the Paul Speratus text, "Salvation unto

Us Has Come." (A point of interest—"Salvation unto Us Has Come" was Luther's favorite hymn.) The confident tune fits the creedal confession of Kingo's Baptism hymn.

Tradition about the Hymn

While there is not a specific tradition that has developed surrounding this hymn, it is sung again and again confidently by the faithful as child and family process to the baptismal font.

The Confession of Faith Sung in This Hymn

There is no other two-stanza hymn so filled with concise, rich statements of what it means to be a Christian. With a few words, it pictures life in Christ from cradle to grave. The confessions made in this hymn include

- Salvation comes from believing and being baptized in Christ.
- Baptism makes a person a new creation.
- The new creation springs forth from the redemption earned by Christ on the cross.
- The newly created child of God joins a glorious company of all peoples from all lands.
- The church prays that, by the Holy Spirit's power, the child will grow in grace each day.

Session 2

Dearest Jesus, We Are Here

Textual Sources:
Psalm 51:5; Mark 10:13–16; John 3:1–21

The Hymn's Text

Pastor Benjamin Schmolck originally wrote this hymn in 1704 as a seven-stanza hymn. He then included it in a work titled "Good Thoughts of the Sponsors Who Journey with a Child to Baptism."

Translation

Catherine Winkworth included a six-stanza translation in her *Lyra Germanica* (1858) and in her *Chorale Book for England* (1863).

The Hymn's Tune

The tune LIEBSTER JESU, WIR SIND HIER was written by Johann Rudolph Ahle in 1664. J.S. Bach wrote a beautiful choral setting of this tune for the congregation as well as various settings for organ. The setting in *Lutheran Worship* is in the style of a Bach chorale harmonization and lends itself to four-part singing.

Tradition about the Hymn

This may be the most commonly used Baptism hymn in Lutheran congregations.

The Confession of Faith Sung in This Hymn

Listen to what Johann Gerhard says concerning what happens at the font:

> The water of baptism is that pool, which heals us of the malady of sin, when the Holy Spirit descends into it and troubles it, as it were, with the blood of Christ. ... At Christ's baptism the heavens were opened; so at our baptism the gates of heaven are opened to our souls. At the baptism of Christ all three persons of the adorable Trinity were present; so they are at our baptism. (*Sacred Meditations* #17)

Session 3

Draw Near and Take the Body of the Lord

Textual Sources: John 4:10–14; 6:32–40; 1 Corinthians 10:16–17

The Hymn's Text

This ancient Latin hymn was written between 680 and 691 and appeared first in the *Bangor Antiphonary*, a rare Irish liturgical manuscript now in the Ambrosian Library in Milan. Legend has it that St. Patrick, Apostle to the Irish, may have had something to do with its composition. The first two stanzas from this early Latin hymn clearly reveal that Christians received the cup as well as the bread in Holy Communion.

Draw nigh and take the Body of the Lord,
And drink the holy Blood for you outpoured.
Saved by that Body and that holy Blood,
With souls refreshed, we render thanks to God.
Salvation's giver, Christ the only Son,
By His dear Cross and Blood the victory won.
Offered was He for greatest and for least,
Himself the victim, and Himself the priest.

Approach ye then with faithful hearts sincere,
And take the pledges of salvation here.
He that His saints in this world rules and shields,
To all believers life eternal yields;
With heavenly bread makes them that hunger whole,
Gives living waters to the thirsty soul.
The Judge Eternal, unto whom shall bow
All nations at the last, is with us now.

Translation

John Mason Neale's translation was published in his *Medieval Hymns* (1851), where the final stanza reads:
Alpha and Omega, to whom shall bow
All nations at the Doom, is with us now.

The Hymn's Tune

This wonderful tune called OLD 124TH first appeared in the Genevan psalter (1551) set to Psalm 124.

Tradition about the Hymn

This may be the most commonly sung Communion hymn in Lutheran congregations.

The Confession of Faith Sung in This Hymn

Gerhard says: "O the heavenly and angelic food of this holy supper of our Lord. O the delightful blessings which He here offers to my soul."

The Lord of all invites us to come unto Him, to draw near and receive the food, the health, the forgiveness here offered in His Sacrament. The one who even numbers the hairs of our head honors us, His children, in an intimate way by the gift of His body and blood in this feast of love. In it He is the bread of life and the fountain of life from which flows living water.

Session 4

I Come, O Savior, to Your Table

Textual Sources: Matthew 11:28–30; 1 Corinthians 11:23–29

The Hymn's Text

This beloved distribution hymn by the German hymn writer Friedrich C. Heyder was included in the first official hymnal of The Lutheran Church—Missouri Synod, *Kirchengesangbuch* (1847). Versions of this hymn have appeared in all successive hymnals. According to the *Kirchenlieder-Lexicon*, the hymn's first appearance was in 1710 with 28 stanzas! The *Kirchengesangbuch* has 21 stanzas, *The Lutheran Hymnal* has 15 stanzas, and *Lutheran Worship* has six stanzas. It is one of the few hymns found in Lutheran hymnals that has a refrain.

Translation

The translation was prepared by the editors of *The Lutheran Hymnal* (1941).

The Hymn's Tune

The tune is called ICH STERBE TÄGLICH. It was found in a 1756 manuscript collection in the Leipzig Municipal Library. The collection contains 295 tunes in four-part settings.

Tradition about the Hymn

It is difficult to retain one's concentration while singing hymns with multiple stanzas. Usually around the fifth stanza one's thoughts begin to wander. Was that not true in the Reformation times, when the authors regularly composed such long texts? Yes, it was true even then, and that is why a procedure for singing longer hymns was in place already at the time of Martin Luther. That procedure is called *alternatim praxis*, alternating practice. The practice would assign specific stanzas to choirs, instruments, and organ so the congregation could listen and meditate on that portion of the text while having a break from singing.

The practice is still common today, particularly on some of the more festive hymns in "concertato" settings available from church music publishers. Longer sermon and distribution hymns would benefit from such a practice, alternating stanzas between men and women, pulpit and lectern sides, children's choir and adult choir, or organ and voices.

The Confession of Faith Sung in This Hymn

This Communion hymn speaks pointedly of our weakness, need, hunger, tiredness, restlessness, yearning—our sinful state. Here the tired singers come to receive the Bread of Life. The communicants are confident they will be made whole at the altar of our Lord. The refrain "Lord, may Your body and Your blood be for my soul the highest good!" ends every stanza with that confidence.

Session 5
Let All Mortal Flesh Keep Silence

Textual Sources: Isaiah 6:1–3; Matthew 26:26–28

The Hymn's Text

This beautiful hymn is the "Prayer of the Cherubic Hymn" from the Liturgy of St. James, where it is used at the beginning of the Liturgy of the Faithful, when the bread and wine are brought to the table. The Greek original is also found in the Liturgy of St. Basil as the Troparion for Holy Saturday morning.

Translation

This hymn was translated by John Mason Neale and R.F. Littledale as the "Prayer of the Cherubic Hymn" in their *Translations of the Primitive Liturgies*. Its present form was translated by Gerard Moultrie.

The Hymn's Tune

This text is usually sung with the tune called PICARDY. It is a French carol tune from the 17th century. The tune is named after a province in northern France. PICARDY was first used with this text in *The English Hymnal* (1906).

Tradition about the Hymn

This hymn is included in virtually all present-day Lutheran hymnals.

The Confession of Faith Sung in This Hymn

The early Greek hymns have a profound sense of reverence. "Let All Mortal Flesh Keep Silence" exudes awe and a beautiful understanding of "the other." Such a confession is most fitting in this hymn. It is all about the presence of Christ and the response of men and angels to that presence. It paints a picture of the power and blessing God provides in His Holy Meal.

Soul, Adorn Yourself with Gladness

Textual Sources: Isaiah 33:6; John 6:35; 10:7-10; Revelation 19:6–9

The Hymn's Text

The first stanza of this hymn by Johann Franck appeared in Johann Crüger's *Geistliche Kirchenmelodien* (Leipzig, 1649) set to the tune composed by Crüger. Exactly when the entire hymn of nine stanzas was written is uncertain. Franck published it in section 1 of his *Geistliches Zion* (Guben, 1672) with the heading "Preparation for the Holy Communion." Franck was a lawyer who authored 110 hymns.

John Julian, editor of the *Dictionary of Hymnology*, states:

> This hymn is perhaps the finest of all German hymns for the Holy Communion. It is an exhortation to the soul to arise and draw near to partake of the Heavenly Food and to meditate on the wonders of Heavenly Love, ending with a prayer for final reception of the eternal feast.

Albert F. W. Fischer, editor of *Kirchenlieder-Lexicon*, states that "Soul, Adorn Yourself with Gladness" is "a hymn of purest metal in consummate form."

Translation

This is a composite translation based on the original translation of Catherine Winkworth in her *Lyra Germanica* (1858) and revised in her *Chorale Book for England* (1863).

The Hymn's Tune

The tune SCHMÜCKE DICH was written by the famous chorale tune writer, Johann Crüger. Crüger was a famous musician, cantor, and director of music in the Church of St. Nicholas in Berlin. He is best known for his collaboration with Paul Gerhardt on numerous well-known hymns.

SCHMÜCKE DICH with "Soul Adorn Yourself with Gladness" is a truly beautiful and appropriate wedding of text and tune. J.S. Bach harmonized the chorale and also wrote a magnificent organ chorale prelude on this hymn.

Tradition about the Hymn

This hymn is included in virtually all present-day Lutheran hymnals.

The Confession of Faith Sung in This Hymn

This hymn paints a picture of a banquet. The hymn is rich in the image of Christ and His bride, the church. Unlike "I Come, O Savior, to Your Table," this hymn does not speak of our sinful and tired state; rather, it describes what it is like to be a guest at this feast. We sing here about the joys, the pleasures, the consolation, and the benefits of partaking in Holy Communion.